PRECIOUS MOMENTS

# My First COMMUNION

## ⤞ A KEEPSAKE BOOK ⤝

*Jamie Calloway-Hanauer*

sourcebooks
jabberwocky

Published by Sourcebooks, Inc.
P.O. Box 4410, Naperville, Illinois 60567–4410
(630) 961–3900
Fax: (630) 961–2168
sourcebooks.com

Source of Production: Leo Paper, Heshan City, Guangdong Province, China
Date of Production: November 2017
Run Number: 5010559

Printed and bound in China.
LEO 10 9 8 7 6 5 4 3 2 1

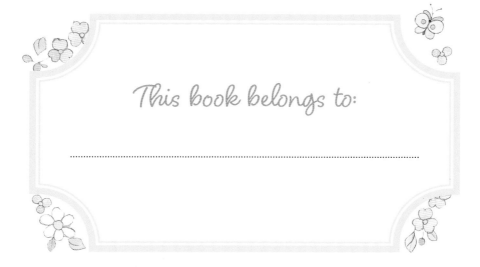

This book belongs to:

........................................................................................................

Then he took a loaf of bread, and when he had given thanks, he broke it and gave it to them, saying, "This is my body, which is given for you. Do this in remembrance of me." And he did the same with the cup after supper, saying, "This cup that is poured out for you is the new covenant in my blood."

**—LUKE 22:19-20**

# CONTENTS

*A picture of me on the day
of my first Holy Communion*

### About My SPECIAL DAY

My first Holy Communion was on: .............................................................

The church where I received my first Holy Communion was at:

.................................................................................................................

.................................................................................................................

My first Holy Communion was performed by: ...................................

.................................................................................................................

The special people present for my first Holy Communion were:

.................................................................................................................

.................................................................................................................

What I remember most from my first Holy Communion is:

...................................................................................................

...................................................................................................

...................................................................................................

...................................................................................................

...................................................................................................

My first Holy Communion was special to me because:

...................................................................................................

...................................................................................................

...................................................................................................

...................................................................................................

...................................................................................................

# Notes from
## MY LOVED ONES

........................................................................................................

........................................................................................................

........................................................................................................

*From*........................................................................................

........................................................................................................

........................................................................................................

........................................................................................................

*From*........................................................................................

........................................................................................................

........................................................................................................

........................................................................................................

*From*........................................................................................

........................................................................................

........................................................................................

........................................................................................

*From* ........................................................

........................................................................................

........................................................................................

........................................................................................

*From* ........................................................

........................................................................................

........................................................................................

........................................................................................

*From* ........................................................

........................................................................................

........................................................................................

........................................................................................

*From* ........................................................

Your First COMMUNION

Congratulations on taking your first Holy Communion! This is a very special step in your faith journey, and needs to be celebrated!

This day is special because it means you have started a new life with Jesus. This relationship started several years ago, when you were a very small baby. Your parents brought you to church and had you baptized in front of everyone who was there that day.

That baptism was how you were first introduced to the Body of Christ, and it was a day when the people of the church agreed to care for you and teach you the ways of faith.

## Joining Your CHURCH

WHEN YOU TAKE YOUR FIRST HOLY COMMUNION, YOU HAVE moved beyond being an infant baptized into the church to taking your first adult step along your journey of faith. You now understand what it means to have a relationship with Jesus Christ. You have chosen to become one with Him by bringing Him into your heart, and receiving His gift of grace. That is why your friends and family celebrate on this day: Your new life with Christ has begun!

To some, the bread and wine or juice of communion are just food and drink—but they aren't. Instead, with prayer and faith and blessings, those simple things—those *elements*—have become Jesus, giving Himself to you.

You were able to take your first Holy Communion because you are old enough to understand how very special that is. You've learned about Jesus and what it means to eat the bread and drink from the cup; you know that Jesus has truly now become a part of you. You may not know everything there is to know about faith, but you know enough to want to receive Christ into your heart and live for Him. You are more grown-up now than you were before, and the adults in your life know it! You will now go to confession as adults do, and you are well on your way to confirmation— full membership into the church.

With communion, you have become a part of the Body of Christ. In fact, that's why it's called communion: You have become part of a worldwide *community* of faith!

# The First
## COMMUNION

TAKING COMMUNION GOES FAR BACK INTO HISTORY, ALL THE way back to the earliest days of the church. The tradition of communion is so old, and so important to the church, that you will someday pass it down to your own children! In fact, it was Jesus Himself who long ago began the tradition of communion. Right before He was to be crucified, He had a meal with His disciples. Jesus knew He wouldn't be around longer, and so He made a point of leaving part of Himself here on earth, so that all who loved Him could remember Him.

The Bible tells us that this is what happened: "Then [Jesus] took a loaf of bread, and when he had given thanks, he broke it and gave it to them, saying, 'This is my body, which is given for you. Do this in remembrance of me.' And he did the same with the cup after supper, saying, 'This cup that is poured out for you is the new covenant in my blood.'"

From that time on, communion became the most important part of Christian worship. In the early days of the church, it wasn't always easy to take communion or even to go to church at all, as not everyone wanted people to experience Jesus's love. But those who loved Him would take communion anyway, even if they got in trouble for it, because they knew how amazing a thing it was to receive His grace.

So you see, your first Holy Communion is an incredible thing worthy of great celebration!

# Living FOR JESUS

Examine yourselves, and only then eat of the bread and drink of the cup.

**—I CORINTHIANS 11:28**

It's exciting to know that you are now taking an active part in your relationship with Jesus. By receiving communion you are saying you want to live for Jesus, and that part of living for Him means taking a look at—or *examining*—the things you do and how you act. That's why you had to have your first confession before your first communion—often when we take a close look at how we're doing things, we realize that we may not be doing them in the way most pleasing to Christ. That's okay—everyone does this! The important thing is that you try your best. That means living in honor, respect, accountability, and faith. Thankfully, we've been given instructions on just how to do this—you can find those directions in the Bible! You can learn a little about them in this book, too.

# ··· Honor ···

When you received your first Holy Communion, it is as if you told Christ that not only did you want Him in your life and heart, but that you would also try your best to live for Him. God will not force you to do this; instead, it's up to you. And that's what honor means: keeping your word to try your very best to follow Jesus.

Remember: God loves us "just because"—there is nothing we can do or not do to earn God's love—but in the Bible we learn that there are some ways that God wants us to live, not for God's sake, but for our own and for those around us. It's up to us if we live

REPORT CARD
Kindness .. A
Mercy .... A
Love .... A
Faithfulness A

teacher

that way or not, but when we take communion and become one with Christ, we're saying we agree to try our best to live the way God would like us to.

Some of the ways the Bible teaches us to live are through acts of "hope, faith, and charity."

# ···Hope···

Hope isn't something we can see or touch, but is something
that we feel. There are times when it's easy to have hope, and
times when it's hard. We should try to feel God's hope
even in those times when it's hard, because

God wants us to know that there is a plan and purpose for our lives, even when things seem tough.

God works in ways that we don't always understand, and that sometimes makes it even harder to feel hopeful. But with belief in God comes hope: You are a child of God, and you are God's beloved.

Think of Jesus and how He died for us. After He died, those who loved Jesus were sad and hopeless. The Son of God was dead. Where was the hope in that? But in their moment of the very deepest sadness, what happened? Jesus came back to life! There was no need to be sad—God had a plan all along!

Remembering this can help keep your hope strong and growing, as can remembering that you are loved, wanted, and protected by God.

# ... Faith ...

Another word very close to hope that we read about in the Bible is "faith." Just as we trust God and feel hope even on our worst days, we also feel faith on those days. In fact, without faith, there would be no hope! Faith means that we believe in God and Jesus even though we've never seen them.

We learn in the Bible not to test God, but rather to simply trust. And that trust is where we find our faith. It's a little bit confusing, but what it is important to know is this: We can't see God, but we can feel God! And even on bad days when we can't feel God because things are just too rough, we keep our faith. And it's this very faith in God that brings us the hope to make it through those bad times.

# ... Charity ...

One thing our faith tells us is that it is through us—God's people—that others get their hope. That's because God's son, Jesus, taught us that the most important lesson of all from the Bible is to love everyone! And when we love people enough to make them feel good about themselves, or help them out when they are down, or give them food when they are hungry, it's that much easier for those we love to feel hopeful!

In the Bible, that love is sometimes called "charity." Charity can mean giving food or money or other things to people who have less than we do, but it can also just mean plain old love.

We all show our love in different ways. We love our family in one way and our friends in another. We love our teachers and our pets and our favorite things in different ways, too. Then there's a bigger kind of love, called *agape* (AH-ga-pay) or selfless love, and that's the kind God tries to teach us about the most, probably because it's the hardest kind there is!

# ... Kindness ...

This love means being kind even when we don't feel like it. Or giving up the last piece of chocolate cake to someone else just because it's the right thing to do. And it means loving people we don't know, or maybe know but don't even like!

God doesn't say we need to be best friends with everyone we meet, but God does say we need to treat everyone around us the way we'd want to be treated. In fact, that's something so important that we call it the Golden Rule: Do to others what you would want them to do to you.

# ··· Respect ···

Sometimes when we love people, we give them hugs and kisses. Other times we love people by being their friend, or helping them when they are sad. Another way we can show love is through something called "respect."

This is probably a word you hear a lot, maybe from school teachers, your parents, or your grandparents, and you hear about respect a lot because it's really important. When it comes to our relationship with God, respect means that we live our life the way Jesus taught us to. It means we read the Bible and act on the things we read in it. It also means that we listen to those who know more about life and God than we do.

Your pastor knows more about God and Jesus and the Bible than you do, and so he is a good person to show your respect by listening to what he tries to teach you. Your parents likely know more about how to live for Jesus than you do since they've been doing it longer, so it's a good idea to respect the advice they give you, too. When you listen to them and do what they say, you are respecting them the way they deserve. But guess what? When you do this, you are also respecting God! Did you know that the Bible tells us we are to respect our moms and dads? It's true! The Bible tells us that when kids listen to their parents, the kids grow up to be happier and better people. But God doesn't leave out kids! The Bible also says that parents should be fair to their kids. That's God's way of giving kids respect, too, because everyone deserves the respect of being treated with God's love!

# ··· Compassion ···

The same is true of compassion. You may not have heard that word before, but it's something really important to know about. Compassion isn't the same as love, but it's close. Compassion is when you see someone hurting and feel that hurt with them. Then you take the love you have for that person and turn it into action by helping to heal their hurt in any way you can. Think of compassion as good works done with love, caring, and understanding, all thrown together to make one big beautiful rainbow of living faith, bringing its beauty to you and to everyone around you.

# ... Traditions ...

One way we can show respect is by keeping the traditions of our faith. Traditions are things that are passed down from generation to generation throughout time, much like communion itself! Other faith traditions include going to church, reading the Bible, praying, and celebrating the holidays that are important to the church, like Christmas and Easter and Lent. When we do these things, we grow stronger in our relationship with Jesus, and we show those around us that we take our faith seriously and that it is important to us. This might even help bring others closer to Jesus, too, which is a great way to show love!

We read in the Bible that God has given us "dominion" over the earth and the animals in it. That means that we are responsible for being good stewards (that's a fancy way of saying caregivers) of the things in nature that God has given to us to enjoy. This is an awesome way to show that we respect God!

# ... Forgiveness ...

Yet another way we can show respect for God as well as for the traditions of the church is to seek God's forgiveness for the things we do that we know we shouldn't. This is such an important tradition that you were asked to seek God's forgiveness through the act of confession before you were able to receive your first communion. That's what it means to confess—to recognize what we've done that we shouldn't have, admit to it, ask forgiveness for it, and then try not to do it again.

It's as if you were trying to hide that you broke your grandma's favorite vase, but instead you went to her and said, "Grandma, I broke your vase. I'm sorry and I won't do it again." It's hard to do, sure, but more often than not, your grandma will appreciate that you were honest about it, and she'll forgive you.

This is also called "accountability." Being accountable means that we make sure that we do what we're supposed to do to live our lives for Jesus, and if we don't, that we admit to it and try again. No one other than ourselves are responsible for our actions, so it's up to each of us to make sure that we act honorably, respectfully, and faithfully in all things. And if we don't, we must not give up trying to follow Jesus! Instead, we need to notice where we've gone off the path and then get right back on it! Your journey of faith is going to last your entire life, and that's a very long time! All the things you're learning about your faith today will still apply when you are your parents' and grandparents' ages. And they'll still apply when you're even older than that! So you have lots of time to practice getting it right.

Remember: There's nothing more important than your relationship with God, because that's the relationship all your others are built on. It's never too late (or too early!) to realize something's gone wrong somewhere, seek forgiveness, then start all over again!

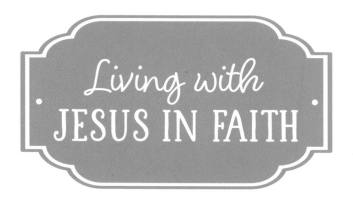

*Living with*
# JESUS IN FAITH

Now that you have taken your first adult step in your walk of faith and are trying your best to live for Jesus, your faith will grow and grow. You will have questions and look for the answers. Sometimes you'll find them and sometimes you won't. But even when you don't, acting honorably, respectfully, charitably, and with accountability will grow your faith in ways you can't even begin to imagine. The Bible tells us that if we even have faith as small as a mustard seed (which is a really tiny thing!), we can move mountains. And you, having taken your first Holy Communion, having been unified with Jesus and accepted His grace, have faith even greater than that seed.

So remember:

- Hope is a powerful thing. When you can look at something bad and find hope in it, you are showing the strength of your faith.
- When you act in love and compassion even when you don't feel it, you will begin to feel love in ways you never expected, and your heart will grow.
- When you do good works—helping a friend or someone in need—you will be bringing the life and love of Jesus into this world, and the world will grow in love.
- With faith, hope, compassion, and charity on your side, you can do amazing things!

# PRAYER

WHILE COMMUNION IS A SPECIAL WAY OF BEING ONE WITH Jesus, prayer is a special way of talking to God. Prayer should become a very important part of your life, as it's our direct line to the ear of God. Some people think it's easy to pray, and others think it's pretty hard. But just like with baseball or playing the piano, the more you practice the better you'll get! Trust that God is listening when you pray, even if you feel like you aren't doing a very good job.

If you want a way to practice, Jesus gave us a great way to do it! He gave us something called "The Lord's Prayer," and used it to teach us to pray.

## THE LORD'S PRAYER

Our Father in heaven,

hallowed be your name.

Your kingdom come.

Your will be done,

on earth as it is in heaven.

Give us this day our daily bread

And forgive us our debts,

as we also have forgiven our debtors.

And do not bring us to the time of trial,

but rescue us from the evil one.

**MATTHEW 6:9-13**

What's great about this prayer is that it has all the different kinds of prayers in it. You might not have known there are different kinds of prayers, but there are! They are called prayers of thanks and praise; intercession; supplication; and consecration/dedication.

# ... Prayer of Thanks ...

A prayer of thanks and praise is just what it sounds like—it's a way to say "thank you" and to give praise to God. It can be something as simple as saying those very words—thank you—and knowing in your heart that you're sending that message up to God, or as complicated as a Psalm, which are songs of praise that we can read in the Bible.

Here's an example of a shorter prayer of thanks and praise from the book of Psalms.

**PSALM 106:1**

Praise the Lord!
O give thanks to the Lord, for he is good;
for his steadfast love endures forever.

See how simple that is?

Here's an example of a longer, more complicated prayer of thanks.

### PSALM 138:
### THANKSGIVING AND PRAISE

I give you thanks, O Lord, with my whole heart;
    before the gods I sing your praise;
I bow down toward your holy temple
    and give thanks to your name for your
    steadfast love and your faithfulness;
    for you have exalted your name and your
    word above everything.
On the day I called, you answered me,
    you increased my strength of soul.


All the kings of the earth shall praise you,
    O Lord, for they have heard the words of
    your mouth.
They shall sing of the ways of the Lord,
    for great is the glory of the Lord.

For though the Lord is high, he regards the lowly;
    but the haughty he perceives from far away.

Though I walk in the midst of trouble, you
        preserve me against the wrath of my enemies;
        you stretch out your hand, and your right
        hand delivers me.
The Lord will fulfill his purpose for me;
        your steadfast love, O Lord, endures forever.
        Do not forsake the work of your hands.

# ... Prayer of Intercession ...

Another type of prayer is called a prayer of intercession. That's a big word that means a prayer asking for God to help someone in need, which is also a way to show compassion. When you see a need, pray for that need and ask God to meet it. How will you know what people need? Sometimes they'll tell you, and other times you'll just see it even if they don't tell you.

Just like with prayers of thanks and praise, intercessory prayers can be big and complicated, or little and simple. For example, when I'm driving and I hear an ambulance siren, I say a very quick prayer, asking God for the person in the ambulance to be okay. I don't know what that person's need is—in fact, I probably don't even know the person!—but I know there's a need. Otherwise the ambulance wouldn't have its siren on!

The Bible tells us how and why we are to offer prayers of intercession. One of these explanations can be found in the book of Timothy.

First of all, then, I urge that supplications, prayers, intercessions, and thanksgivings be made for everyone, for kings and all who are in high positions, so that we may lead a quiet and peaceable life in all godliness and dignity. This is right and is acceptable in the sight of God our Savior, who desires everyone to be saved and to come to the knowledge of the truth.

**1 TIMOTHY 2:1-4**

The Bible also gives us examples of what the prayers might sound like. This is a very pretty one from the book of Philippians, in which St. Paul is praying for others to grow in their relationships with Christ:

And this is my prayer, that your love may overflow more and more with knowledge and full insight to help you to determine what is best, so that in the day of Christ you may be pure and blameless, having produced the harvest of righteousness that comes through Jesus Christ for the glory and praise of God.

**PHILIPPIANS 1:9-11**

# ... Prayer of Supplication ...

There's also a special kind of prayer when you pray about you and your needs. It's called a prayer of supplication, and it's probably the most common type of prayer there is. Have you ever asked God to help you get out of trouble? Or to do well in a game or on a math test? Those are prayers of supplication! Sometimes prayers of supplication are longer and more serious. These prayers are sometimes very much like having a conversation with a good and trusted friend.

In fact, we read in the Bible that when you are asking God for something, it's a lot like asking your dad, because you know you're talking to someone who loves you very much:

> Ask, and it will be given you; search, and you will find; knock, and the door will be opened for you. For everyone who asks receives, and everyone who searches finds, and for everyone who knocks, the door will be opened. Is there anyone among you who, if your child asks for bread, will give a stone? Or if the child asks for a fish, will give a snake? If you then, who are evil, know how to give good gifts to your children, how much more will your Father in heaven give good things to those who ask him!
>
> **MATTHEW 7:7-11**

Here is an example of a prayer of supplication from the book of Psalms:

### PSALM 86:1-7

Incline your ear, O Lord, and answer me,
for I am poor and needy.
Preserve my life, for I am devoted to you;
save your servant who trusts in you.
You are my God; be gracious to me, O Lord,
for to you do I cry all day long.
Gladden the soul of your servant,
for to you, O Lord, I lift up my soul.
For you, O Lord, are good and forgiving,
abounding in steadfast love to all who call
on you.
Give ear, O Lord, to my prayer;
listen to my cry of supplication.
In the day of my trouble I call on you,
for you will answer me.

# ... Prayer of Consecration ...

Another type of prayer you should know about is prayer of consecration, also called a prayer of dedication. This is a prayer when something or someone is consecrated—or dedicated— to the Lord. As you were preparing to be given your first

communion, you heard a prayer of dedication from the pastor. He blessed the bread and cup and dedicated it to the service of the Lord. It is through this act that the elements become holy. These prayers are common in the Bible, as people dedicate themselves, their towns, or their children to God. Here's just one example from the Bible, which also talks about prayers of petition.

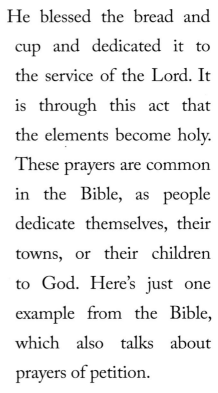

And she said, "Oh, my lord! As you live, my lord, I am the woman who was standing here in your presence, praying to the Lord. For this child I prayed; and the Lord has granted me the petition that I made to him. Therefore I have lent him to the Lord; as long as he lives, he is given to the Lord."

**1 SAMUEL 1:26-28**

## BLESSINGS

ANOTHER GREAT THING TO LEARN ABOUT IS BLESSINGS. GOD loves to give us blessings, and the Bible is full of them! A blessing is an offering of God's grace and protection. Of course, you already have God's grace and protection, but a blessing is a special way of noting that in a certain way.

The Bible offers us words of blessing from both God and Jesus, and teaches us that, as children of God, we can offer blessings, too! When we give others a blessing, we are using the authority—which is a sort of power—that we have been given by God to spread God's love here on earth. We often say blessings before meals, blessing even the food we eat so that we can be strong and healthy.

There are so many blessings in the Bible that we know they must be very important! God wants people to know they are cared about, and what better way than to give them a special word of love? Sometimes we feel bad about things, even ourselves, and hearing a blessing from someone might be just the thing to make us feel better.

As someone who has been baptized and has taken communion, you are able to give someone a blessing! Remember, this is not a blessing you are giving from yourself, but rather a blessing you are giving of God's protection and love.

The Bible lets us know that we should try to be a blessing to everyone, so feel free to give a blessing to anyone!

You can make up your own blessings, but here are a few from the Bible to get you started:

> And God is able to provide you with every blessing in abundance, so that by always having enough of everything, you may share abundantly in every good work.
>
> **2 CORINTHIANS 9:8**

> The Lord bless you and keep you;
> the Lord make his face to shine upon you,
>   and be gracious to you;
> the Lord lift up his countenance upon you,
>   and give you peace.
>
> **NUMBERS 6:24-26**

> May he grant you your heart's desire, and fulfill all your plans.
>
> **PSALM 20:4**

# · BENEDICTION ·

A SPECIAL KIND OF BLESSING IS CALLED A BENEDICTION. A benediction is special because it's a kind of "sending." That means that it's a blessing that sends you out into your day to do God's work in the world with God's divine protection over you. At the end of church, a pastor might give the congregation a benediction to stay with the people throughout the week, hoping that they feel the love and protection of God, and that they share that with others, so that others may come to know God as well.

Here are a couple of benedictions from the Bible:

The Lord be with your spirit. Grace be with you.

**2 TIMOTHY 4:22**

The grace of the Lord Jesus Christ, the love of God, and the communion of the Holy Spirit be with all of you.

**2 CORINTHIANS 13:13**

May grace and peace be yours in abundance in the knowledge of God and of Jesus our Lord.

**2 PETER 1:2**

As you can see, these benedictions are very simple, but they offer a whole lot of love!

And now the time has come for the final benediction, as you embark on your journey of faith, living your life for and with Jesus Christ.

May God love and protect you, offering you every good grace. May you offer this same love and grace to others, bringing the spirit of God with you wherever you may go.

You are a loved and wanted child of God. Go forth and be a blessing!